I0071846

THE OBSERVATION ENGINE

THE OBSERVATION ENGINE

TARA GENTILE

Copyright © 2015 Tara Gentile

All rights reserved.

ISBN: 0692510656
ISBN-13: 978-0692510650

DEDICATION

Dedicated to Sean McMullin,
my partner and friend, who has taught me the value of
observation in a whole new way.

CONTENTS

INTRODUCTION

What if you could take the guesswork out of marketing? What if you could take the guesswork out of sales? What if you could take the guesswork out of turning ideas into great products?

As it stands right now, you likely face fear after the euphoria of a new idea wears off. You don't know if this precious new idea is going to succeed or fail. You don't know if you'll be able to make people care about it.

You do know how many different tactics you've tried in developing new products that still always feel like a bit of a crap shoot. You've rushed things to market to beat off the competition. You've acted on assumptions about price or customer limitations just to try to get it right. You put so much effort into marketing campaigns, sales conversations, and product development only to have customers balk at the financial value of what you've created.

They don't see how your idea changes things for them. They don't see how they can put it to use right now. Of course, it's not their job to see it. It's your job to show them.

This is a tiny book about making your big ideas matter. It's about ensuring that every idea you bring to market is welcomed, used, and adored. This book shows you how to build and use a system I call the Observation Engine to understand your customers' current state of affairs and connect it to the ideas you want to share with them. An Observation Engine is a purposeful cycle of listening, examination, and response that turns simple observations into powerful information that fuels your business's product development, marketing, and sales.

Through the kind of collaborative and systematic processes involved in an Observation Engine, you can all but eliminate the guesswork in how you bring a new idea to the people who need it most. You'll spend less time in development, less money on marketing, and less heartache on the sales process.

1
MAKING IDEAS MATTER

I've been studying idea-driven businesses for over 6 years while I've been building my own. I watched companies like Evernote and MailChimp constantly adjust their product and messaging as their communities revealed new layers of value, need, and meaning. I witnessed companies like Etsy and Groupon squander goodwill and make decisions that alienated their bases.

It quickly became apparent that the businesses that succeed develop a careful cycle of perception, alignment, and reflection. They observe what is most important to their prospective users, they align their products and campaigns accordingly, and then they learn from the results. They use this cycle to fuel their product development, marketing, sales, and customer engagement activities. These businesses see "social" not as an unrefined broadcasting tool, but the ultimate research and development department.

Social isn't about media; it's not even about business. Social is about being human: listening more than talking, observing more than philosophizing. As Nilofer Merchant explains in 11 Rules for Creating Value in the Social Era, "Too many still see social as the purview of two functions: marketing and service. It's either 'Like us on Facebook!' or 'We're so sorry you're having a problem.' While a few have figured out that they can use social to listen to the market—sort of like putting a stethoscope to the market heartbeat—there is more to this social thing."

What people talk about or create through social media is what matters most to them in the moment. It's the ultimate look at what they care about from minute to minute. When you know what's most important to your users, you can create products, marketing, and sales strategy that reflect it.

Listening and observing through social media allows you to identify what ideas are going to be the most relevant to your users. (Note: I'll use the term "user" or "prospective user" throughout this book in place of "customer" or "client." The idea of use rather than consumption is an important part of reimagining the people who purchase your products or services in the Social Era.) The most relevant ideas are those that are directly connected to the present reality of prospective users.

If your ideas don't speak directly to your users' reality, you have some work to do. That work, of course, is marketing.

Marketing is the process we use to connect our ideas to what's current and important to prospective users— their present reality—and turn our ideas into relevant ideas. Most product ideas aren't relevant. They require marketing to make them relevant and give them meaning. Marketing is what gives context to your idea so that others understand why they should buy it, even why they need it now. When a business's attempt at marketing is focused on the product idea instead of ideas that are relevant to the potential user, it falls flat.

In other words, if you can't see how your product fits perfectly into the lives of the people you want to buy it, they won't either. And they won't buy it.

Whether it's an impulse buy or a planned purchase, we don't buy things that don't fit into our lives. When Steve Jobs introduced the iPod, he made it relevant: 1,000 songs in your pocket. When you land on the Wordpress.org homepage, they make it matter: build a beautiful website or blog for free. When you walk into Chipotle, they show you why it's one of the fastest-growing fast food chains in the US: wholesome food that fits into your busy life.

These businesses understand how their potential users' reality contributes (or not) to the resonance of their ideas. Without resonance, there is no purchase. Resonance is your job as a marketer, entrepreneur, and idea generator.

Resonance is when something just feels right. When an idea echoes what you're already feeling, a circumstance you find yourself in, or something you see coming on your personal horizon, that idea resonates with you. You're tied to it. You give it weight and meaning.

Marketing so often misses that mark. But it doesn't have to.

Steve Jobs could have said the iPod was a miniature hard drive capable of storing 5GB of data. Wordpress.org could say it's an open-source content management system. Chipotle could just position itself alongside all the other fast food restaurants and point to giant burritos.

They don't. They create resonance.

These businesses take users' present reality as inspiration for marketing that resounds with meaning, emotion, and urgency.

You can too. I'll illustrate the process, which I call the Observation Engine, throughout this book. Here's the gist:

- Build systems for making and recording observations

- Identify and describe potential users' present reality
- Create content that tests hypotheses about relevant ideas
- Connect relevant ideas to product ideas
- Adjust product ideas to create more resonance
- Create opportunities to test product ideas

Note that an Observation Engine is not just about marketing. In fact, it's not really about marketing at all. It's about how marketing and sales have become integrated with product development.

Apple didn't set out to create a miniature hard drive and then figure out how to market and sell it. The marketing and sales strategy was built right in by virtue of the way Jobs saw prospective users' present reality and the way he could make it better. Wordpress.org didn't set out to be a content management system; it set out to help people share their ideas on the web. Chipotle didn't set out to be just another fast food option; it wanted to be a better option for busy people.

These companies made decisions about the very nature of their product based on the problems, goals, frustrations, or desires they witnessed their prospective users dealing with. Without even knowing it, these future buyers acted as collaborators on a product that would be more useful to them than if it had simply been born out of secret meetings and closed doors.

Your product ideas are also born from real life experience of your future buyers problems, frustrations, and goals. However, in the process of development and refinement, you likely lose track of what you're trying to accomplish for your users. Instead, you're focused on what you want to share with them, teach them, or help them understand. It's not that this focus is misguided; it's just that it doesn't lend itself to compelling marketing or messaging. When your focus shifts to always asking why your ideas matter to your users, you know you're integrating great marketing into the entire product development process.

We've already established that marketing is what connects prospective users to relevant ideas. Sales connects relevant ideas to problems that can be fixed or goals that can be achieved through a product. Without understanding how your product idea connects to a problem or goal in your users' present reality, and how you can use relevant ideas to connect potential users to how your idea can solve that problem or achieve that goal, you won't be able to sell your idea. Successful product development, which leads to effective marketing and sales, creates the necessary resonance with users at the deepest levels.

Marketing and sales are not activities that come after a product is fully formed and ready for public use. Marketing is not just promotion. It doesn't come after product development, nor is it dependent on it. Sales strategy is not something that's decided on when the product is rolling off the assembly line. Marketing, sales, and product development are inextricably tied.

In today's business world, everyone is a marketer, a salesperson, and a product designer. Whether you self-identify as an idea person, problem-solver, innovator, designer, creator, or developer, you have to keep those 3 disciplines in mind in order to be effective.

Building an Observation Engine allows you to do just that.

ᴛʜᴇ OBSERVATION ENGINE

	TARGET CONVERSATION	PRESENT REALITY	RELEVANT IDEA	PRODUCT IDEA	RESONANCE
SOCIAL MEDIA	identify & join	observe	test	test	measure
CONTENT MARKETING	add your voice	reflect	expand	expand	create
PRODUCT DEVELOPMENT	offer solution	offer alternate reality	incorporate	iterate	enhance
PROMOTIONAL CONTENT/ADS	become the topic of convo	connect	connect	connect	connect
SALES	influence	influence	influence	exchange	capitalize

Before we go further, I'd like to define some terms I'll be using throughout the book (and a few I've already used), which you can also see in the Observation Engine graphic above. I've decided on a specific vocabulary for the Observation Engine because I'm recasting so many words (like marketing and sales) that have accidental synonyms and popularly misconstrued meanings.

By defining a set of terms for this system, I hope to give you a fresh perspective on what's possible for your business as you take the guesswork out of your marketing, sales, and product development.

Target Conversation

"Markets are conversations," says *The Cluetrain Manifesto*. We talk a lot about the importance of researching our target markets, but I find it more helpful to understand your target conversation. Joining that target conversation is a big part of your Observation Engine, as is observing the other people participating in it and the other businesses creating in it.

Knowing your target conversation, more so than even your target client or target market, helps you know where to look for clues about your prospective user is experiencing right now. You can witness the shape, language, and emotion of a conversation. You can also interact with it and see how others respond.

Present Reality

Your prospective users are surrounded by certain circumstances and focused on certain goals. They feel things, wonder about things, and try to get where they want to go. Their relationships, emotions, situations, questions, and concerns all shape their present reality.

If you ignore any part of your prospective users' present reality, you run the risk of missing the connection between what they're experiencing and what you're offering. One of the goals of your Observation Engine is to collect as much information on your prospective users' present reality as possible.

The focus is on the present because your product idea aims to change their reality by solving a problem or achieving a goal. Once you've done that, you'll have a new present reality to gather information on and use in your marketing, sales, and product development strategy for your next product idea.

Relevant Idea

A relevant idea comes from the target conversation. It's your response to a question, a misconception, a fear, a goal, or an issue that people are talking or asking about. When you craft an answer to what people are already talking or asking about, your idea suddenly becomes relevant.

You can't make someone care about your product idea just because you love it so much. You might think your product idea is an obvious solution to a pressing problem. But if it isn't clear to prospective users how your product idea fits into their beliefs or worldview (not to mention their schedules, skill sets, or budget), they won't buy it. The relevant idea you use to connect your product idea to your customers shows them how it fits in.

Product Idea

Your product idea is probably why you started reading this book in the first place. Sure, you want to take the guesswork out of marketing—but for what purpose? Your product idea. You've spotted a problem and created a solution. Or perhaps you have an idea and desperately want to share it with others.

Or maybe you fall into the smaller camp of readers who are interested in building an Observation Engine in order to find a product idea.

Either way, your product idea is what you're creating to be of service of others and create value.

Resonance

When you create content to respond to the conversation with the answer to a question or the solution to a problem prospective users' are dealing with in their present reality, you create resonance. People feel "in harmony" with what you're broadcasting. They choose to tune in instead of tuning out.

The more your content creates resonance in the market, the more people will be actively paying attention. The more people pay attention, the more they'll talk back to you and inform the rest of your marketing, sales, and product development strategy.

In *To Sell Is Human*, Dan Pink calls the ability to create

resonance attunement: "Attunement is the ability to bring one's actions and outlook into harmony with other people and with the context you're in." In context of your Observation Engine, your "actions and outlook" are the content (social, promotional, etc...) you create, the methods you use to promote what you have to offer, and the messages you use to sell it.

Messaging

Messaging is the idea behind your sales process. It connects relevant ideas to the users' present reality and their present reality to your product idea. When messaging creates resonance, prospective users are much more likely to buy.

2
WHERE IT ALL BEGINS

In order for people to buy your product, it has to matter to them. The idea behind the product has to mean something to them. Even the smallest purchases we make are made to create change, comfort, or ease.

You make an impulse purchase when your present reality triggers the desire for something that will (as you perceive it in the moment) make you happier or more comfortable. For instance, last night while I was buying a sandwich, I picked up a pack of gum from the impulse area by the cash register. I needed the sandwich because it was dinner time; that's why I was at the store in the first place. I impulsively bought the gum because my present reality was that I was boarding a flight to Montana in about 10 hours. Gum helps me avoid motion sickness and keeps my ears from popping. To me, flying means buying gum to stay comfortable.

New products and marketing campaigns fail when they fail to connect the product idea with the present reality of the prospective user. The connection between most product ideas and the present reality of their users is not as simple as buying gum before a flight. Consider Evernote, a note-taking and organization application.

Right now, I'm writing this book in Evernote. In fact, I'm an Evernote super user. I've written all of my books in this app, I take all my client notes in this app, and I even manage projects using this app. But why Evernote, when my computer comes with a default text editor and a word processing program, and the internet is full of tools specifically designed for project management?

Because Evernote has search. It's available for all of my devices. It's easy to use yet robustly featured. I can share notes with my whole team or with the public. I can set reminders and chat with team members. All of these features add up to one incredible value: I can remember everything.

Evernote keeps me from that devastating feeling of having a brilliant idea only to forget it an hour later. That could be my present reality: I could feel forgetful and unproductive—and often have. But with Evernote, I don't.

Evernote took my present reality—constantly forgetting ideas that make me happy, make me money, or connect me with others—and tied it to something I want much more: to remember everything. A less savvy marketing department would list all of Evernote's features and try to compete on how those features differentiate it from traditional word processing tools and text editors. But Evernote's marketers kept it simple. They tied my present, forgetful reality to the ultimate outcome.

Evernote took their idea and made it resonate.

I work with "idea people." I'm an idea person. We like ideas. No—we get obsessed with ideas. So obsessed, in fact, that we often ignore the world around us in favor of diving deeper and deeper into our own ideas. This is the main factor in the most common reason that product ideas and marketing campaigns fail: we obsess over our own ideas at the expense of clearly communicating why they should matter to others. When we don't (or can't) clearly communicate why they should matter, it's impossible to create resonance with your marketing, sales process, or product.

You put a new idea into the world, you promote it as much as you can, and no one cares. The idea doesn't get traction. Sure, some people will buy, but they're just a fraction of the total market that could buy if only they understood why the idea was useful or delightful.

Of course, this is a recipe for disaster when it comes to getting your great idea into the hands of the people who need it most. I've weathered my fair share of those disasters, as have my clients. To avoid disasters like those, I created a system for observing and understanding the present reality of my prospective users.

It used to be that observing your customers' present reality and starting a dialogue with them about their desires, frustrations, and problems was expensive. You needed to devote countless resources to research and development, and then you needed to devote more resources still to broadcast-style mass marketing. It cost a lot of time, money, and energy to take a new idea to market in a way that it could actually be successful.

This is no longer the case. The advent of social media and the connected age has made it virtually costless to observe and interact with the people you want to buy your ideas. You can build communities, galvanize movements, or simply woo the right people with a blog post or video.

I'm sure it's not news to you that most businesses are entirely focused on what they can create or broadcast with social media instead of its most potent use, observation. Your potential users are out there; they're creating photos, videos, and updates. Are you paying attention? Are you asking yourself what it means when a media trend pops up in your feed? Are you (or your marketing department) spending time immersing yourself in the present reality of your potential users?

The most potent use of social media for a marketer is observation, not broadcast. When a marketing message is grounded in what the marketer observes as the potential users' most pressing desire, problem, or frustration, one update get the same results as 20 updates. Observation creates efficiency.

Observation allows your every broadcast to be signal, not noise.

Curation and Context

There are two key aspects of applying your Observation Engine when it comes to social media: curation and context.

Curation is how you make sure you're paying attention to the right information from the best potential users. Every social media channel has a way to curate its feed or interface so that you're seeing the information you most want to see. By eliminating the distraction of non-relevant information, you can be reasonably confident in the validity of your observations.

Context is essentially what you're looking for in your curated feed. There's the context for how your potential users are addressing their present reality, the context of how they're talking about their problems, the context of how they're feeling about what they want to accomplish, and so on. If as a marketer you can perceive the precise context around how your product idea is likely to be received by the user, you're much more likely to create marketing campaigns that resonate immediately.

To start curating the way you observe potential users, create a Virtual Focus Group. Your Virtual Focus Group is a small group of people who represent the archetype of your ideal user. Better than an ideal client profile, your Virtual Focus Group are real people, not assumptions or generalizations. You can find your Virtual Focus Group by looking back through your past customers of existing product or choosing target users for a new product idea.

Start small. I ask my clients to pick 3-5 people to focus on at first. As your understanding and facility with your Observation Engine grows, you can add more people to your Virtual Focus Group.

Once you have identified your Virtual Focus Group, you can create curated feeds in the social media where they post most often. This could be a custom feed on Facebook, a private list on Twitter, or a playlist on YouTube. If it's not possible to create an automated curation feed on the channel your users frequent most often, you can set up bookmarks that allow you to quickly visit the content they're posting.

This is the very beginning of your Observation Engine. The content you're observing sheds light on the present reality of your users and offers valuable insight on what matters most to the people who matter most to you.

Social media invites people to create content about

what matters most to them in the moment. Sometimes that's lunch, other times it's a political issue, still other times it's a personal problem, a health issue, or a professional concern. All of this content creates context for you as the observer. Depending on your field, what your potential user thinks about a political issue may be less important than a pressing health issue—or it could be just the opposite.

All context is valuable by a matter of a degree. If you're targeting entrepreneurs who also happen to be mothers and you're ignoring the context of their children's activities, you're going to miss big opportunities for both marketing angles and product innovation. If you're targeting single 20-something men and you're ignoring the context of how much time they're spending on dating apps, you're missing out on the potential for powerful partnerships.

It's not your job to sift through what you observe to find the relevant parts; it's all relevant. It's your job to look for how the context you observe is connected to your product idea. Sure, you will discard some of those connections as you craft your overall strategy. But to discard them before you craft a strategy sets you up for a lot of wasted potential.

Once you've curated your feeds and have started taking note of the context of your potential users' present realities, you need to record your observations in a useful manner. The tool I use and recommend for this process is called a Perspective Map. Your Perspective Map is an extremely simple contextual tool that allows you to make connections and mine insights you might not have otherwise noticed.

A Perspective Map is a simple 4-quadrant grid. Starting in the upper left and moving clockwise, label the 4 boxes Say, Do, Think, and Feel.

To begin filling in your Perspective Map, identify the problem, desire, or frustration your product idea addresses. If you don't know what that is exactly, no problem. Start by considering the change your potential users are looking to make. What is it they'd be trying to accomplish by purchasing a solution? Again, even the simplest of impulse buys help customers accomplish something, even if that something is fleeting.

With that problem or change in mind, scour your feeds for evidence of what your potential users are saying, doing, thinking, or feeling about this problem or how they think they should solve it. Keep in mind the important question first posed by marketer Gene Schwartz, "What do your customers already know?" This is the key to understanding how to approach your prospective users. They may be completely unaware of their problem but still seek to alleviate distress, discomfort, or inconvenience. They might have a misunderstanding about what their actual problem is. They might be on the right track with their problem and have no idea how to solve it. Or, they might be completely aware of potential solutions to their problem and are seeking a way to understand which solution provider might be best for them.

What your potential users say and do about their problem or desire is observable. What they think and feel requires you to engage your social brain. In the same way you can infer what a friend is thinking or feeling from the things they're sharing with you, you can infer what your potential users are thinking and feeling about the problem your product idea solves.

Fill out the Perspective Map grid in as much detail as possible, always taking the perspective of your potential user, never your own.

Let's look at the Evernote example again to see the Perspective Map in action. By curating their feeds, Evernote marketers might see that their potential users are talking about their big ideas, how their body of work is evolving, and what new insights they're excited about. They might also share how they've been using Google Docs to share information with their team, managing projects with Asana or Basecamp, or communicating with coworkers on Slack. The Evernote marketers could infer that their potential users prefer to stay organized and productive, that they value efficiency, and that they prioritize creative output even more. They feel defeated when they forget a great new idea and excited when they stumble on something new.

From here, Evernote could explore several marketing angles. They might try a content marketing campaign centered on "Productivity + Creativity = Results." Or, they might highlight their sharing features by choosing an ad campaign that focuses on "Great teamwork turns good ideas into great ones." Or, they might end up with the campaign that hooked so many of my friends and clients (and me!): "Remember everything."

3
YOU DON'T KNOW UNTIL YOU TEST

Taking the guesswork out of marketing, sales, and product development doesn't mean you'll always get it right straight out of the gate. Testing and experimentation is a key component of your Observation Engine. Once you get information about the present reality of your prospective users, you'll want to look for the relevant idea that will connect your product to their lives.

There are lots of relevant ideas for your prospective users, and many paths for connecting their lives to your product. Using what you initially observed, you might spot several questions your marketing could answer or a key misconception you could refute in a sales call. But you won't know which is the best until you test those ideas.

You can use content marketing and social media to experiment with relevant ideas so that you can see which elicit the greatest response, how the response might affect the path you use to connect the idea to your product, and even what complementary ideas could strengthen your marketing and sales strategy.

To begin testing, start with one of the questions, misconceptions, or problems your prospective users are talking about. I'll share an example from my own business to illustrate. In summer 2014, I started experimenting with a new relevant idea. I was promoting a workshop I was running on CreativeLive, an online learning platform, about marketing and launching new products. From observing my target conversation, I knew that one of the greatest fears my users had was coming across as salesy, shouty, and obnoxious as they were promoting their products.

Anticipating this fear, I had used the phrase "quiet power strategies" in the description for the workshop. I wanted people to know that they could use what I was going to teach even if they didn't want to be self-promotional. Revisiting that workshop description, I thought "quiet power strategies" might be a relevant idea, but I wanted to test it.

I created content using the idea and it took off. I kept creating content and observed how people interacted with it. I noticed what resonated, what fell flat, and what was misunderstood. These short posts would take just a few minutes to put together but resulted in tons of priceless information.

As I learned more about how and why "quiet power strategies" resonated with my audience, I incorporated the idea into the very workshop I was promoting. The work I did marketing my workshop actually influenced and improved the workshop itself.

Finally, the Quiet Power Strategy idea turned into a book and led to a rebrand of the largest segment of my business. Relevant ideas don't just connect users to products; they inform the product you're creating. Just as you don't know what marketing angles are going to be a hit with your audience until you test them, you don't know how your final product will look and act until you test your marketing.

Almost all product ideas evolve as they make contact with their users, so you save time, energy, and heartache when those ideas touch your potential users as soon as possible. Instead of waiting until your product idea is ready to be made public, present your ideas in the form of content: blog posts, social media updates, emails, videos, events, etc. This way, your ideas make contact and start evolving sooner, making your product idea stronger as it too evolves.

This is the essence of joining your target conversation. Promotional posts and ads don't do much to further the conversation; they rarely catch users' attention. When you present relevant ideas that respond to the conversation that's already happening (and it is already happening), your ideas become part of something bigger, something organic, something real. If you're passionate about your idea or serving your users, this should be welcome information: resonance is your goal, not unceasing promotional coverage. It's not about how many email blasts you can send out or even how many sales calls you can make; it's about how much resonance you can create as you join the conversation.

Earlier, I mentioned your users' level of awareness. Different users are aware of their problems in different ways. They talk about different things. It's likely that the conversation your business needs to participate in doesn't use the same language you're using to talk about your product, but this is an important detail to consider. Look at travel rewards credit cards. Providers like Chase don't talk much about low APRs, balance transfers, or flexible spending. Instead, they talk about fewer travel blackouts, more rewards points, and dream vacations. The conversation they're participating in is about travel, not finance. The relevant ideas they use to connect to their users are travel ideas.

When Alec Baldwin was the spokesman for CapitalOne's Venture card, CapitalOne used two relevant ideas: "Fly any airline anytime" and "Double miles you can actually use." They observed their prospective users talking about how restrictive other reward programs were and countered with improvements to their own program and marketing to highlight the differences. The ads didn't depict Baldwin balancing his accounts; they showed him traveling by plane or vacationing on a tropical island.

This might seem obvious—the connection between what matters and what you're selling—but missing that link is probably the most common marketing mistake I see businesses make. The quality of your idea, the innovativeness of your approach, the forcefulness of your message—none of it matters if your potential users don't see why your product matters in terms of what they're struggling with, working towards, or trying to achieve, big or small. This connection to what matters is resonance, and it's what leads to sales.

Another way to look at resonance is simply whatever makes your potential users feel on the verge of getting what they want. To create resonance, then, you need to know what your prospective users want. What they want is probably not your product, especially if it is new, innovative, or forward-thinking. You can't want something you don't know exists.

The burden is on you as a marketer to create resonance—which in turn creates desire—for your product.

4
RESONANCE MOVES PEOPLE

I used to live in a small town on the Oregon coast, about 2 hours west of Portland. My access to hip or professional clothing was extremely limited, yet for public speaking and teaching, I needed to refresh my wardrobe often. That meant a lot of trips into the city or a lot of online shopping returns.

When I heard about StitchFix, I knew I needed to try it. StitchFix is "your partner in personal style." When you sign up, you create an individualized style profile that helps a real live human stylist choose clothing they think you'll love. They send you 5 pieces on your schedule, you keep what you want, and you return the rest. You pay nothing up front and there's almost no risk.

For women who regularly need (or want) to refresh their wardrobe with pieces that can't be found in big box stores, it's a godsend. I've requested pieces for a speaking engagement in Cancun, stage-worthy dresses for a teaching gig, and comfortable jeans for everyday life. Today, most of the clothes I wear have come from StitchFix, courtesy of my personal stylist.

When I signed up for StitchFix, I wasn't looking for a clothing subscription service. I wasn't looking for anything in particular, really. I just had a need for new clothes. StitchFix engineered both their marketing and their product to meet my needs in a way that created extreme resonance. They had observed the problems that come with traditional shopping (like lack of access and fear of trying new things). They also observed the trend for sharing your personal style online through blogs, Pinterest, and Instagram. They created resonance by merging their potential users' needs with their natural behavior.

Then, they met those potential users where they were in attempting to meet their own needs. StitchFix leveraged Pinterest, Instagram, and Facebook to share their message, their product, and—most importantly— great content that stoked the passions of their potential users. They also used these platforms to encourage users to share their own experiences and successes with the service. In fact, the first time I heard about StitchFix, it was from a user and blogger who was raving about the clothing she'd received.

Too often, marketers and idea people are too

concerned about trying to get the word out about their product. They think the more people they can reach with the name of their great idea, the more people will buy. "If only more people knew about my product, my business would be more successful," they say. This couldn't be further from the truth. It's not how many people know about your product; it's how much it resonates with the right people.

One way to find your path to resonance is to acknowledge that your potential users are already trying to solve the problem your product idea solves. For StitchFix, that means recognizing that their potential users are trying to find great clothes even if they don't have great places to shop. How are they doing that? They're driving to bigger cities, they're placing massive orders at online retailers hoping to find a few things that could work, or they're making do with cookie-cutter fashion. To create resonance with a promotional post, video, or photo, all they need to do is acknowledge these problems.

Imagine a video that shows a box being delivered via FedEx. A young woman answers the door and collects her box. She opens it to reveal that she's ordered 2 styles of dresses… in 3 sizes each. It's not so much an exciting online purchase as it is a lottery. She tries each on and is out of luck, both with size and style. She then struggles to return it all.

If you've ever tried shopping this way, you're all too familiar with this scenario. You immediately resonate with the woman's frustration.

Now, the video transitions and the music picks up. The next shipment that arrives is a small robin's egg blue box. The young woman answers the door again with a smile on her face. She actually has no idea what's in the box, but she's excited to find out. She opens it and tries on her items, mixing and matching them with items she already has in her closet based on the outfit cards that are included in the box. She decides on 3 items and drops the other 2 in the pre-addressed self-adhesive bag that was inside the box. The last frame of the video is the woman confidently walking into the office the next day in her new clothes.

This video will create resonance with any potential user who has tried to hit the online shopping jackpot. Of course, you could create similar videos with the other solutions they've tried—one where the woman shows up to work in the same outfit as a colleague or one where she hops in the car for a 2-hour road trip to the mall only to get frustrated with the whole shopping experience.

The point is that marketing needs to start with a situation, feeling, or experience that feels incredibly familiar to the potential user. When you lead with the features of the product, and even when you lead with the benefits of the product, you run the risk of missing the mark and having the customer not understand why your product matters. Instead, when you show the potential user a snapshot of her own daily life and how your product fits into it, you've eliminated the chance that she won't see why she needs it. You've taken the guesswork out of making an impact on your potential user with your marketing.

Resonance moves people. It gets them to pay attention. It's what triggers that feeling of "Wow! That's exactly what I've been looking for" even if they've never considered the kind of product you've just showed them. Resonance turns familiarity into desire.

5
RESONANCE DRIVES
PRODUCT DEVELOPMENT

If your marketing lacks resonance and you don't see a clear path to creating a more moving message, it's likely that your product needs to change. Iteration and evolution is a natural part of the product development process. And, since creating a product that is easy to market and easy to sell makes sense for efficiency and profitability, it fits that you want to determine your path to resonance as quickly as possible.

When your marketing strategy is unclear or nonexistent, you can edit the product to make it more resonant. If you're too precious about your product idea, you can very easily miss the chance to create something that really makes an impact. Eric Ries writes in The Lean Startup: "Every entrepreneur eventually faces an overriding challenge in developing a successful product: deciding when to pivot and when to persevere." If your biggest challenge in developing your product is crafting marketing that resonates, it's likely time to make a pivot—even if it's a small one. Fitting your product idea into your users' present reality is an opportunity to take a different angle, look at necessary features from a fresh perspective, or adjust the context of the idea by applying a new lens.

Even if your product is successful and your marketing strategies create resonance, product iteration is still an important part of the Observation Engine. Take another look at Evernote. When Evernote realized that users were sharing their notes and talking about their content with colleagues and team members, they made note sharing easier. Their observations helped them recognize an opportunity for resonance and pointed the way to a new feature (Work Chat)—which in turn allowed them to create fresh messaging to court more prospective users. Then, Evernote created Work Chat. While this feature, in my opinion, requires further development, it nonetheless represents a big step forward in how Evernote's product connects to the reality of their users.

Often, entirely new products or revenue streams are born from your Observation Engine and the continued quest for resonance. When one of my Quiet Power Strategy™ clients, Shawn Fink, was searching for a way to grow her business, we started where we always start

—by observing her potential users. Shawn is the creator of The Abundant Mama Project, and when we started working together she'd already led hundreds of customers through her personal development and awareness program for moms seeking mindfulness. Our goal was to create a strategy to double her revenue; the easiest way to do that was to create additional value for women who were already sold on her brand.

Shawn observed that, after the revolutionary experience of The Abundant Mama Project, her customers were looking for a way to maintain their new lifestyle while enhancing their relationships with themselves, their partners, and their children. As mothers ourselves, Shawn and I knew that it was hard to make meaningful life changes and that the support of a community could help maintain those changes. That difficulty to make changes would be the point of resonance, and a monthly subscription would be the product.

Soon after, The Peace Circle was born. The Peace Circle allows alumnae of The Abundant Mama Project the opportunity to continue interacting with like-minded mamas, improving their new skills, and ensuring that the meaningful changes they've made stick. The offer has been easy for Shawn to market because, based on her observations, she already knows that "change is hard, friends make it easier" is a relevant idea for her potential users. Shawn built the product with the marketing in mind, allowing resonance to drive the creation of a whole new revenue stream for her business.

Marketing is not something that happens after a product has been born. It's an integral part of product development, and your Observation Engine helps to ensure that the product you're bringing to market is the product people want to buy. When you use marketing to inform your product development process, you have multiple paths to resonance, which leads to greater success both on the financial and the impact levels.

6
HOW TO BUILD YOUR ENGINE

Your Observation Engine is a system. But it's not a system in the sense that it has a clear process or procedure. Instead, it's a conglomeration of actions, touch points, experiments, and impressions that fuel and power your business. At any time, you might be using social media to observe the present reality of your potential users, enhancing your product by upping its natural resonance, and connecting a new audience to your relevant idea through promotional content.

Abby Covert, author of How to Make Sense of Any Mess, writes, "When we jump into a task without thinking about what we're trying to accomplish, we can end up with solutions to the wrong problem. We can waste energy that would be better spent determining which direction to take." Such is the problem with the actions we take when it comes to social media, content marketing, product development, promotion, and sales. But when we know the purpose of our action—and the potential next step—we can build efficiency and effectiveness into our daily work instead of wasted energy. Using the Observation Engine graphic, you can plot your next move based on where you're at with product development, marketing tests, or sales conversations.

THE OBSERVATION ENGINE

	TARGET CONVERSATION	PRESENT REALITY	RELEVANT IDEA	PRODUCT IDEA	RESONANCE
SOCIAL MEDIA	identify & join	observe	test	test	measure
CONTENT MARKETING	add your voice	reflect	expand	expand	create
PRODUCT DEVELOPMENT	offer solution	offer alternate reality	incorporate	iterate	enhance
PROMOTIONAL CONTENT/ADS	become the topic of convo	connect	connect	connect	connect
SALES	influence	influence	influence	exchange	capitalize

Social Media

Many marketers today are putting huge amounts of energy into interacting with users and creating content for social media. While analytics for these activities are improving every year, much of this energy is still spent without proof of a real return. When you utilize social media as part of your Observation Engine, you can better direct your actions and use the output to fuel the rest of your engine.

You can identify and join your target conversation through social media. If you want to know what people are talking about, asking questions about, or just generally sharing, look at social media. Direct your observations toward the platform that your potential users are most likely to use; each one has its own flavor and demographic leanings.

Once you're into the target conversation, use social media to observe the present reality of your potential users. If you only pay attention, they'll tell you what they're doing or thinking about. Once you know their present reality, you can find a relevant idea and begin to test it. Posting links, asking questions, or offering tips are great ways to engage people with your relevant idea. You can do the same with your product idea by offering sneak peeks. Once you've shared your relevant idea or product idea, you can measure resonance by observing the way people talk back or share.

Content Marketing

Content marketing encompasses the blog posts you're writing, the videos you're producing, and any other way you're curating or creating stories or information for your audience. Content marketing allows you to add your unique voice to the target conversation and reflect on the present reality of your potential users to nurture your relationship with them.

Content marketing also allows you to expand on your relevant ideas and product ideas after you test them in social media. You can go further in depth or offer additional insight. Finally, you can create content that allows you to create resonance with your potential users by reflecting on their present reality, expanding on your relevant ideas, and connecting the two together.

Product Development

Products can't be just great ideas; they need to be a solution to a problem—no matter how big or how small. Within your target conversation, there is a lot of opportunity to see problems, desires, frustrations, and inconveniences that can be addressed through product development. By carefully observing your target conversation, you might spot new ways to develop old products, openings for new products, or ways your existing products could improve.

The goal of your product development in terms of your users' present reality is to show an alternate reality. Every step of the process should be geared toward making that alternate reality easier for them to accomplish. One way to do that is to incorporate your relevant idea (how you're connecting the product to the users' present reality) into the product itself. Look for opportunities to use your relevant idea in the features and set up of your product. Then, as your relevant idea evolves to reach more people, your product development can evolve in turn. Your relevant ideas and the ways you're creating resonance inform the process of iteration so that you can enhance your product's natural ability to connect with users.

Promotional Content/Ads

Advertising and promotional content are designed to make people aware of a specific product they can buy. One of your chief goals with promotional content should be to become the topic of conversation in your target conversation—the very definition of viral marketing.

When it comes to your users' present reality, your relevant ideas, your product idea, and the resonance you create, promotional content is about connection; an ad that connects with viewers sticks with them when they go shopping and influences their future purchases.

Sales

Sales is all the action you take to actually make a transaction happen. As I mentioned earlier, it's connecting an existing problem to the product you're selling so that your potential users know to buy it. Your goal with sales is to influence the target conversation so that people are talking about the right problem, to influence their present reality to help them see new possibilities, and to influence their ultimate buying decision so that they start using your product.

Marketing is preparation; sales is the follow-through.

Through sales, you initiate financial exchange—or, in other words, you finally make money on your product idea. And through sales, you finally capitalize on all the resonance you've created.

No matter where you are in the process, there is no "end." Your Observation Engine keeps running. If it stops, so does the forward progress of your business, as your product development, marketing, and sales start to grind to a halt. If you are trying to create new results for your business—whether a new product, a new marketing campaign, or a new sales strategy—you can reference the Observation Engine graphic to source an action that gets your engine humming.

Revving Your Observation Engine

Start with where you're at. If you're already in product development, look for your next step. Maybe you know you need to create content marketing in order to generate interest in your idea. Work through your options in Content Marketing and turn your observations into enhancements for your product. Perhaps you're trying to create promotional content or ads for an existing product. You can use Social Media to grab the information you need to work your way through the Promotional Content/Ads section.

On the odd chance you're starting from scratch with a new business or venture, start in the upper left corner (Social Media/Target Conversation) and work your way out, both right and down, as you begin to cover all the activities mentioned in the graphic. You'll need to work several parts of the system concurrently to get the most benefit. Luckily, many usual business tasks can be incorporated into your Observation Engine so that the very act of running your business revs your Observation Engine.

Ultimately, your goal is to capitalize on the resonance you create. Resonance is valuable. It helps us identify who we are, belong to communities both local and dispersed, and figure out how to solve old problems in new ways. When your business capitalizes on resonance, it's capitalizing on something long-lasting and profound. And when you learn how to observe the world around you for the purpose of creating resonance, you have a skill that will serve you for years and years to come.

CONCLUSION

How much more revenue could you generate if you took the guesswork out of your product development, marketing, and sales? How much more time could you save? How much more ease could you find in your business?

With as much sway as product development, marketing, and sales have over your business, you don't want to leave them to guesswork. You need a system. Building and engaging your Observation Engine means that you're never far from your next breakthrough—and the follow-up actions that turn that breakthrough into customers, dollars, and growth. With the Observation Engine, your campaigns aren't flukes, and your sales wins aren't blind luck.

If your business has been struggling to make its mark

or if you feel like you've been trying to find your momentum for too long, it's time to crank your Observation Engine.

ABOUT THE AUTHOR

Tara Gentile is a business strategist and the author of Quiet Power Strategy and The Art of Earning. She works with entrepreneurs and idea people to help them leverage their Quiet Power and build businesses that generate wealth, peace, and ease. Her clients learn to lead themselves and their businesses based on what makes them most effective and compelling.

She's the founder of Kick Start Labs and the creator of the Quiet Power Strategy™ business coaching program.

Tara's work has been featured in Fast Company, Forbes, Design*Sponge, and in the New York Times bestselling book The $100 Startup by Chris Guillebeau. She's a regular instructor on CreativeLive and speaks on entrepreneurship, money, and the New Economy all over the world.

OTHER BOOKS BY TARA GENTILE

Quiet Power Strategy

The Art of Earning

The Art of Growth

ACKNOWLEDGEMENTS

Thanks to Amy Scott, founder of Nomad Editorial, for editing this book. Thanks to Breanne Dyck for helping me shape the way I communicate ideas. Thanks to the Quiet Power Strategy community for continuing to influence my methodology.